Sm
Shopping

By Becky Gold

CELEBRATION PRESS
Pearson Learning Group

Tomato
#1.69

Contents

Ready... Set... Shop Smart!

People are often in a hurry. They can rush through chores with very little planning. Sometimes people rush when they go food shopping. They often spend too much money. They don't always get the best products. They spend more time than they would if they weren't in a rush! Does your family shop in a hurry?

Being a smart food shopper takes effort. You need to understand some math ideas. You need to take the time to use the ideas. Smart shopping is worth the extra time, though. It helps you get the things you need at the best prices.

Stores can be confusing. Smart shoppers come prepared.

How does smart food shopping work? Most people buy their food in supermarkets. These big stores are filled with a huge number of **items**. What are the best prices? Where do you find them?

$1.69 lb.

Here's where smart shopping pays off. To be a smart food shopper, you need to take your time in the store. Compare products to get the freshest food. Compare prices, and watch the cash register to save money. Get ready to help your family shop smart!

$2.99

$1.59

Smart shoppers learn how to compare products and prices.

Smart shoppers use **coupons** to save money on the items they purchase.

What's in Store?

When you go into a supermarket, take a good look at the **layout**. Are displays placed up front where they'll catch your eye? Store managers want the displays to be the first things you see. They may be filled with snacks, toys, or other costly items. You may want to stop to check the displays out. Keep moving! Remember, you only want to buy what you need.

Tips Before Shopping

- Before shopping, write down what you need.

- Take this list to the store. Only buy the things on the list.

- Don't shop when you're hungry. You might buy things you don't need.

A shopping list can help you to buy only the items you need.

When you shop in a big store, look up! Signs hang above each aisle. The signs list the aisle number. They also tell you what you can find there. Similar items are grouped together. For instance, pasta and spaghetti sauce are usually found in the same aisle.

Read the signs to make your shopping trip faster and easier.

Knowing where items are found can help save time when you shop. Take a notebook with you on your next shopping trip. Write down the aisle numbers and what products are in each aisle. The next time you shop, you will know exactly where to go. You'll save time.

layout of a typical supermarket

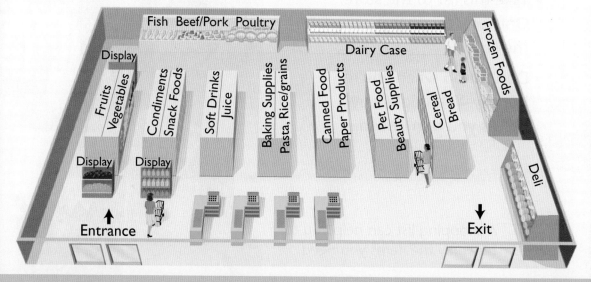

Dare to Compare

Smart shoppers do **comparison** shopping. They don't grab the first item they see. Instead, they compare brands.

How can you be a comparison shopper? First, look at prices. Look at sizes, also. Sometimes, buying larger sizes of a product saves you money. You can get more for your money than you can when you buy smaller sizes.

When You Comparison Shop...

- Check prices. Higher-priced items may not offer the best value.

- Check freshness. Many products are labeled with **expiration** dates or "sell-by" dates.

- Read the list of ingredients on food items. Is this product good for you?

- Check the weight or **volume** of the item. Is it as much as you need or more than you need?

Supermarkets sell many different brands.

7

For most people, price is important when deciding what to buy at the supermarket. Comparing prices can make you a smart shopper.

Items in a supermarket are priced in different ways. There is the **individual** price, such as the cost of a single loaf of bread. This price can be found either on the product or on the shelf sticker.

Possibly the most important price to look at is the unit price. This is also listed on the shelf sticker.

unit price   individual price

The unit price shows the cost of an ounce, pint, pound, or other amount of an item. It can help you compare the cost of products that are sold in different-size containers. It is the best way to compare the price of two products.

In the example below, two boxes of cereal have the same total price. However, you can buy 18 ounces of Tasty Wheat for the same price as 12 ounces of Crispy Wheat. The difference is the lower unit price for Tasty Wheat Cereal. It costs $0.20 per ounce, while Crispy Wheat Cereal costs $0.30 per ounce.

Check the product price, the unit price, and the size of the items you want to buy.

	Unit price (per ounce)	Size	Total price
Crispy Wheat Cereal	$.30	12 oz	$3.60
Tasty Wheat Cereal	$.20	18 oz	$3.60

A Weighty Matter

As you compare prices, also note how much you are getting for your money. Find out how products are measured. Then, compare. Two boxes of cereal may be the same size, but the amount in each box may be different. For example, one box may contain 11 ounces. Another box may have 12 ounces. If the boxes are equal in price, buy the box with more cereal.

Weights and Measures*

Number Amount used for items such as eggs
- 1 dozen = 12
- half-dozen = 6

Weight used for dry goods such as bread and pasta
- 1 ounce (28.35 grams)
- 1 pound = 16 ounces (454 grams = 0.454 kilogram)

Volume used for liquids such as milk, oil, and juice
- 1 fluid ounce (29.57 milliliters)
- 1 pint = 16 fluid ounces (473.18 milliliters)
- 1 quart = 2 pints = 32 fluid ounces (0.95 liter)
- 1 half-gallon = 2 quarts = 64 fluid ounces (1.9 liters)
- 1 gallon = 4 quarts = 128 fluid ounces (3.8 liters)

*metric amounts are in parentheses

More Ways to Save

Another smart shopping idea is to think of buying things in **bulk**, or large quantities. A bulk price is usually lower than an individual price. However, be careful about buying in bulk. Make sure you can use the amount you are buying. Try to choose items such as pasta or canned foods that do not spoil easily.

Individual Versus Bulk Prices

Compare the individual and bulk prices below. Which do you think is the better deal? (See answer on page 16.)

Product: Paper towels
Individual Price: $2.00 for 1 roll
Bulk Price: $10.00 for 10 rolls

Less Is More

Next time you're in the store, look at the packaging of bulk items. Cereal may come in a large bag instead of a box with a bag inside. Less paper and plastic may be used. So, if you buy in bulk, you may help the environment.

Another way to save is to buy **generic** items. These are also called store-brand items. They come in plain packages. They are not advertised on TV or in magazines. Ads cost a lot of money. They try to make you think name-brand products are better. This isn't always true. Generic items are often just as good and are less costly.

Fancy Versus Plain

There are other ways to compare prices and shop smart. Take a look at a product's package. For example, does the more expensive spaghetti sauce come in a fancier jar? The cost of the package is part of the price you pay.

Don't pay more for a fancy package!

Check the Shelf Life

Did you ever buy a carton of milk that smelled sour in just a few days? You may not have checked the sell-by date. This date tells you the last day you should buy that milk to get the freshest milk possible.

You can also find an expiration date on many products, such as canned soup. It tells you when a product is no longer safe to use, or **consume**. Remember to check these dates. Then you'll be sure you are getting the freshest and safest products for your money.

Sometimes items with later sell-by dates are stored in the back of a row. Be sure to reach behind the front-row items to get the freshest products.

How Long Will It Last?

Here are some recommended shelf times:

apples	1 to 2 days on the shelf/ 3 weeks refrigerated
carrots	2 weeks refrigerated
cereal	1 to 2 months opened
grapes	1 to 2 days on the shelf/ 1 week refrigerated
lettuce	1 week refrigerated
milk	1 week refrigerated
poultry	1–2 days refrigerated
rice	1 year opened

Check It Out

Are you ready to check out? Your job is not over yet. Here's what a smart shopper needs to know at the checkout.

- Watch the cash register display. Make sure the prices on the screen are correct.
- Give the cashier any coupons that you have. Try to use coupons for brands you would buy anyway.
- If the cashier makes an error, say something.
- Always check the charges on your **receipt**.
- Count your change to make sure it's correct.

The next time your mom or dad goes to the supermarket, ask to go along. Gather your coupons. Bring a notebook and a grocery list. Take your time, and have fun being a smart shopper!

Smart shoppers check out the checkout!

Glossary

bulk   a great size or amount

comparison   looking at what makes two or more things the same or different

consume   to use up

coupons   pieces of paper that can be used to save money on a store item

expiration   ending time; an expiration date is the date at which a product is no longer safe to use

generic   without a brand name

individual   single

items   separate things that are part of a group

layout   the way a space is laid out or arranged

receipt   a paper that lists purchases and the amount of money paid

volume   the amount of space inside a container that has a length, a width, and a height

Index

answer to question on page 11: The 10-pack of paper towels is the better deal. You pay $1 per roll, or $10 ÷ 10. If you bought 10 single rolls at $2 each, you would pay $20 for them (10 × $2), or twice as much!